Nowhere Nearer

Nowhere Nearer

First published 2018 by
Liverpool University Press
4 Cambridge Street
Liverpool
L69 7ZU

British Library Cataloguing-in-Publication data
A British Library CIP record is available

ISBN 978-1-78694-102-2 softback

Typeset by Carnegie Book Production, Lancaster
Printed and bound in Poland by Booksfactory.co.uk

for my father, Peter

We are no longer quite here and not yet there at all.

Anna Freud, Vienna, 1938

Contents

Saving

Any time there is a window, or a winter, or a news
report strung out to minute-by-minute;

Any time there is a letter, a philosopher, a question of
travel through time or Wien; any time there's a claim

we can learn to stretch our minds across the greys of this
    precise universe
which itself slouches in an infinite series

of likewise or elsewise universes;
Any time someone reaches down to pick up a copy

of the *New Yorker*, and it is March 2008, and this
gesture changes their whole-life-plan because of a poem

by W.S. Merwin which says (among
other things) that all flowers are a form of water

and the whole world's burning;
Whenever our hands touch like swords

and we bow, either because we want
to obey the rules of combat

or because it might help to save our necks;
Whenever the blue hour;

Whenever fathers wait for children
to arrive on a plane

when even the 24 hour news cycle
has had to admit the story is over

with the wreck fished out
and no survivors;

Whenever I promise but send you nothing

what I am failing to say

is that some of the moments we cling to most
are the futures we never let happen.

Out of this World

In Vienna the young
woman kicks at a fence at the station, waiting
to catch a train out of the world. Digital sign says no train's due.

Out of the world or out of the mind?
On this weak-lamped morning, I watch
the woman kick the fence, which, after a fit of
persistence, falls. What loveliness
increases, what passes, what woman
now standing on tracks staring down
the train. Blazed light.

She is too far for anyone to reach her.

Is it like picking up an instrument and beginning to play.
Is it like a smattering of false similes, fooling foreignness into
    feeling familiar.

Man on his back hugs guitar like a lover,
but will not play a note.
The woman makes no more noise.

In creased hills, rubbled grass,
in rocks scattered like blades,
I see the country I'm from,
though I'm so far nowhere
nearer. No nearer death,
no passing train. The world's
stealing all the leaves again, leaving
notes in a language I don't read.
Because this fence guards nothing
but dark weeds and smashed glass
this morning I have kicked it down. The digital sign
says nothing's coming.
No time to count down.

Observatory

Across from the observatory,
under cream cloud, what is it
death does when it undoes—the gradual unravel of a brain,
or a switch's flick to click off thought?

Before me, I love the muddy canal,
love the fact that before Dante
enters Hell he meets a leopard.

I see leaves and a giant lamp
made to resemble the moon. Hung above
the observatory. Clouds pull in more clouds.

How easy it is to glance and see nothing. How easy to spend
our time puzzling how to spend our time.
Young boys run past, serious for their bodies,
and in a breath of heat and sweat they're gone.

Night comes for the ten thousandth time, sky growing
muddy with cloud, light squeezed out.
Are you there, a man says into his phone.
A magnificent storm is coming.

Zentralfriedhof

Would you like to visit a famous grave?
Good. Sit down. Admire your future:

burned bones, green furred stone. Remember being part
of an empire? Good. It is something you will

tell others while you live. It is something you will say
you belong to. The songs they are singing on the mount

are no longer yours, but that does not matter.
Do not look on anything, do not despair.

You will ask to leave here soon enough.

How to Remember

I moved to Freud's town for you,
although 'for you' was too much to say
at the time. I said we moved
together. I moved, for once,
for something other than myself.

Other than myself! Can that be right?
The story they tell of this city
is you never see the inside.
You're kept out so adeptly you see only
stage sets, not even the true outsides of the walls. You only
hear it spoken of enough to want it. Once I heard cues
for the side show, never the main event.

Since you left me I walk around here a lot.

I'm not dead, either. To be not dead,
I claim, is the most marvellous thing in the world.
Or to be touched, to have a finger pushed inside you.
Some people are approaching in Chinese dragon masks,
and twisting their way through a rehearsal. People hold their
scripts and do not know their hands shake.

We borrowed stage sets we can shift, paint, switch,
but now we will never see the main event.
What we see will always disappoint us.
Reality does what it likes. I am not dead, we say.
Nothing is being done to me.

No one's skin on mine.

In my brain's city, I built a lot of skyscrapers.
I am a hoarder. I press all things around me
so I can't tell the things from myself.

In that brain's city, we are still a unit. We clip
our tickets, open doors with silver keys,
pour coffee into glasses, and read about other city's atrocities.
We stroll through the supermarket like Orpheus, singing in
     our tiny Hell.

How well done it was, what we did.
How good we were at all of it.
Inside the city the courts declare the election
must be held again, red curtains reopened,
script wholly rewritten,
and now the people applaud.
They are proud to be part of something strong
enough to push people away.
The sun hinges in a willow between stage lights
and no one can move it.
The dragon is made up of twenty people all of whom
have a different idea of what a dragon wants.

It never lasts, didn't we know already?
It keeps not lasting.

City you are always here to remember it by.

(Dear then, when less was known, and the sun
rose by itself, was not hauled up by hand,
how did we not see this coming?)

In this field you can't find the instruments
you brought to speak to ghosts – there's only
this dead stone tower
crumbled alive with crawling
ivy – you shut your eyes but instead
a Shetland pony presses her nose
against your pockets
and will not leave
till she has found and swallowed every crumb.

On a picture I took of the path
that was empty

after a deer had crossed it:
thunder like airplanes; deer

prints like the rattle of dice; fog strewn
like cotton through mills;

leaves shiny as shoe soles.
Each simile soft, anachronistic.

Heavens. Open. Rain.

Last you see is horses.
Sprung with veins and numbers

branded on their backs. The grown ones
with muscles large as human children.
They graze under a bronze statue
of a soldier killed by sword (this is some years
before the musket's introduction). Last you see
one foal rubs his nose
against this statue's base.
A mare near you reaches her own white head

down and last you hear's
that grass, as it's ripped out of the ground.

Europe

Today,   you say,   and all the stones can hear you
each building with its ankles, nape,   and bones
watches with its stone-eyes for your footsteps and holds its

                                        converts
closer to its dome   they listen to sopranos who've trained

                                        years
to glide a flightless note through this stone sky –

but we will not feign a smoothness,
we'll *push past*, like a kid impatient, refer to others'
rhythms of breath, *beyond* our shifting
grain of skin and eyes – because today,

     you say, another man was buried
(*push past*) and the stones may hear but only we
speak back. And we are unsolved
and unsalvageable
and when we go we cannot take our ruins.

What's Gone Blue

Five am in Amsterdam, canal reflects bridge till
windows go mirror. This morning I've
gone full blue while cranes sit high
on skylines. Somewhere creatures fall
in love, their blood rushing 'round their body's canals
and the trees around us all fall too.
We are too sensible, we say. We have love, need
not fall. No one's gone. No one falls.

Plain Tongues

We cobble up a language on the fire
forge words for *voll* and *leer*
for sense and sound,
for song is *sinnvoll*. Signs are soulful, unless sent
from cities we've not sanctioned. Stop singing,
it confuses. We must speak in our
plainest tongues, from our palest our
silkiest bodies. Listen to famous mouths
for our messages. We will never complicate
our meanings. We'll make all clear,
in small words from spun worlds.
You won't even know we're here.

As the Crow Flies
the Sun Rips Day Open

As the crow flies the sun rips day open
to blast rays in stone lions' mouths.

Past the gate with holes like a language,
past the stone teeth that wait for night.

The language of gaps is now
what all the lucky ones learn.

Near Theseus the tram's squeak turns
to squeal but no one looks up;

we're too busy giving
our footprints to the snow.

The crow has found a dead dog
and rests her beak upon its head.

We've bought a history we do not want
and we must watch it every day

until the minutes crack.
The crow eats, and day shakes

her bright head from the frame.

Boy

When they found the boy's body in the river
there was no sign of where he'd come from
his cat-gut hair sprawled to cover
the rock cut through his cheek

I'd heard about him on the train home from work
around where the tracks pull to the left
to avoid the abandoned quarry. No one knew the kid. I
    remember
some lady had brought a baby on the train who screamed

the whole way. Like it had a demon in it squirming
to get out. Those days we didn't get
what it meant, really, to find a dead boy with twigs
and threads still trailing from his arms. We could tell

it was a tragedy of a kind. But we were headed home
to glue our own strong cotton to branches, cut
from the forest where the wood was
the best for miles; we were still holding

out our arms and waiting for the glue
to dry, thinking, maybe, some day soon
we'd get to test our wings.

The Roof

On the roof of an art academy in America, the midterm
    elections
don't touch tourists, the politicians for a few days allowed
to fade to silhouette
in a country not glad to see us, but
at least it's not sad, at least it won't obsess
about its own tide, as we do. When a psychoanalyst
says adults have no notion of home, a
nomadic woman says *rubbish*
and in America rubbish perches on gutters
and won't wash down. A gull has a sense of home?
A bumblebee is bumbling home?
We bumble but we do not gull, only
cull our belongings as we wait to board
    our next plane out. In our bold age. In our bumble back
        to riches and our gull back to rags.
To know we can't know's when
we find the roof's clock tower with six ropes
suspended from its top, pigeons long flown,
one man singing as he loads the bell. The bell, because
now we prefer our music simpler
than our words, because the bell can set the sun
in view of a country we only ever visit
but make believe's our own. Now we too can set
the sun; forget what earth's made of, send
our quick-fingered-work off-
shore. The surprise
change in the tastes we've known
all the time we've had a body; has the taste slipped;
have we? All I know's to go outside
each time a storm breaks, for the first
sleet, fist-sized hail, the cloud

that takes our shadows, the rain-thwacked-
roads; to break open the lie
     of the brainsafe screensaver,
          the lie of clear skies, of stars.

Eva Braun in Linz

Last sun's got that gold,
need not wrestle.

Lazes with a patience, a way that knows language
is a diagram of sound, and violence

can be gentle.
Of course she didn't come here

but it's her I think of, throwing her head back
on a balcony, to flaunt her laugh in colour
for the camera –

as I pass farms, industrial areas, reservoirs –
a small town
with one church at its centre,

the beaten down straw, the neatly ploughed lines
tunnels black as you'd hope for.

Auden's disowned poem says *Find
what occurred at Linz*

so I watch for the billowing imago
I watch for the camp he ordered made

where they tested
what the body, what the mind

could stand – and did you know
he planned to return here?

It was to be his mausoleum?

Leafless trees black out the hill
like a man with a dark head of hair

unbalding. A man with a dark head
who came from here, where the bells chime

and the stones still stand
and the horses shake their heads.

Are we sorry they set her up with him?
Would she have preferred to stay nameless, live longer,
or to be one of the ones who blinked
when a bomb hit a building, for her body,
along with the others, to begone?

Instead, for her, the Berlin bunker,
where he held
a massive model of this very city.

Last sun catches lines
made in fields by machines
after the houses have fallen
in shade
until I can see cyanide in bare trees, in tunnels,

I see so many eyelids flipping open, shut.
Last splash of cloud bleeds gold, turns dull

save one last river where the trees haunt the light.

Yellow

Too much night in the Vienna woods, trunks crumble
into the faces of boars. Boy up
all night reading about crises,
his milk skin dated between the eyes,
the way scepticism twists skin.
I see you in buildings, I say.
I see you in red foxes that
scatter through jeweled woods outside
Chernobyl. In the light
jutted through clouds which don't rise
but curve round like (just say it) heaven.
The child twists her bedsheets.
Turn the night out, she commands.

My Girl in California

In the train, the rain stops to take stock
of what I've kept: a shot of her, a dress,
a wink, a message under
a fake teak bar saying I'll see you in Vienna
when we're calm   which we never are
and just now with the train track's clunk
dusty streetlamps start to pass
their string of streaked lights spread:
one light tries to grip a window – one laughs –
one smudges I love you, takes too long to leave.
Last one finds me, the only one who knows to stare
straight into night.
Otherwise it burns you up. I'm building a temple
to seven types of forgetting: it quotes greats,
lates, and quarterbacks. It whistles to
the night, filled with birds I've fed for years,
tuis, grackles, crows
who dive one-by-one into the Lethe
because they need no memory but their breed's.
We bob birdlike on that river,
but must not dive. We watch
the waves as they shrug from us, feather-
by-feather, light-by-light.

St Peter

The disease in Peter's hand meant
he could not stretch his fingers and so, the story goes,
subsequent popes blessed with the same
fingers' crumble, some digits stretched up,
some clenched in.
    What can we make with our hands?
Never quite what we wanted. Never quite the dead reborn
nor the words as we heard them, never the second's
slippage, nor the human call.
    Tonight people sleep in the open air, die there,
and though we try, our imaginations
cannot make them us.
I throw up my hands, we say, or
my head is Hell enough.
We crush our fingers together.
This is all we can make.

The Soldiers

We picked apples to decorate
the table, not to eat. Pretty till
we let them rot. The men came back
from France next morning, no song, their own
silent rot fingering their feet. Skin pulled apart between
bones. We caressed their empty uniforms.
We filled their handkerchiefs
with rotten apples, watching outside's
laundry's wet-shroud-flap. We clutched
their dead hands and promised never
to let the new wars bloom.

Palace

In the tiny crypt of Diocletian's Palace
Santa Lucia is surrounded
by notes for instance *please*
take care of my father or *thank*
you for our life here.
Everyone's feet ache on the steps of the bell tower
and the man has been looking for hours but cannot
find the temple
of Jupiter. He has been looking all morning and now
he is sick of the pale stone squares on the ground.

Nearby a guide avoids the word Christian
so as not to admit a ruin's newness.
Two men raise their phones
to snap Santa Lucia
in her lake of letters. This place is like a maze,
a woman says. The man decides if he doesn't
stumble across the temple soon
he will look at it on the internet in his hotel room
even though he has already today referred
to the hotel's internet policy as *draconian.*
At least he can say he was there.

If there is anything you have forgotten you can ask me how it
     was,
says Jupiter. In the temple he holds one palm out
with fingers gnarled upwards, still stuck
holding the globe he's lost.

Outside Vienna

All these years I'm still
surprised by snow. This morning,
how it appears on lawns
and rooves, a layer of cloud
for the sledders who cluster
like enormous puppies in luminous hats.

I guess some unlined part of me's still left
in a snowless city singing Māori songs
where tide covers stone, cuddles
shingle, and a creature in the pine needles
chews through the cotton singlet
I buried one evening in the garden;

or sitting in that shitty park god knows how
far from the sea, eating
the Midwest's version of Middle Eastern
food, still drunk from the night before
and caught between the kind of crying
and laughing where you can no longer hold
your eyes open. This morning

inside other mornings, as the city nests
inside other towns, the sun steps in
to blast the snow back
so my eyes must shut,
see only blood.

Neutral Air

Off the Ringstraße, by the hotel
you died in, a screen
shows each week, a new opera.

It calls itself HD but is blurred.
It won't say what poetry makes. This is no time
like your present; this town forgot

most of your century, which killed archduke
then empire then put up plaques to
forget you, for you are

nowhere near. I know that now.
I climbed to the top of the hotel's stairs,
looked down, heard no screams, no voices.

Today there is no opera.
We love one another, we die, what laziness will save us?
What brinks?

Woman

The burned moss is tight on the ground.

Too tight to own its own
shadow. Too long

since the morning's hallway leading down
to the locked room, where green

afternoons stay unseen. I am
what exactly, the woman says.

She won't go back to the room.

*

A moment earlier
with the man's knee bent, the honey
ring's glint,
she looked up, not at him, but at the stone's façade
behind, where rock scrunched, crumbled
under her live gaze. She knew she should speak

but was thinking
robbers came here, marauding
and raping, taking what
they fancied. They fled and she'd like
to flee too, to take what she liked and begone. She wished
she weren't greedy but she also thinks
who's not greedy with time's a fool.
She has seen a creature in the burned moss
and it resembles her,

far more than a kneeling man ever could.
She crouches as the other women walk in slippers,
she waits to watch them

stroll, their hair fall
and shine the outer layer of
a lemon rose. I am so determined

she said to make a
shadow even when
I'm dirt. The man nodded

although he understood nothing.

*

An ant's legs rattle under the leaf's edge,
onto the moss burned yellow – it's been a hard

summer, though easy for him, who does not
have to bother about fields. She will keep

bothering, liking the fresh breeze
of decision. The window creaks,

open-shadowed trees make cameos
in the reflecting glass.

The burned moss pushes back at the feet and knees
of the woman as she crawls, it pulls water from her

soles, her skin. It drinks. Soon
the man will return with his armed guards

but none of them will find her.
The moss slices itself open

and the woman crawls inside.

How to Forget

In Leopoldstadt by the station the drunks
piss in the open air. The Polizei prowl.
I called this place clean when I got here.
It is, relatively speaking. But it can take time to see dirt.

Like a kid at a window asking
how centuries fold and unfold,

how this crow stands now, un-cautious
un-concerned by interruption

determined no matter
how close you get

she will not fly.

How today in a haunted town
the rain is patient
and windows promise
to split our faces

How today in a hunting ground
we tell our stories in the only
wayward inadequate way
anyone knows how

And which parts will you remember best?
In German remembering's reflexive
Ich erinnere mich
to remember something
you must first remember yourself:

so it is easier to forget:
ich vergesse, es vergesst, wir vergessen.

How we repeat ourselves so faithfully
acting the parts we think we made
and echoing those who've come before

how much we need new ghosts to follow

And in his essay on forgetting, Freud
changed the verb *to forget* – so each time
we forget, we must forget ourselves:
ich vergesse mich –

and his editors silently corrected the proofs
forgiving what they saw
as his forgettings.

A match strikes between
what we feel for those we know and
the bewilderment of strangers

When of all the crowds to listen to
it's the dead who know the most

I thump my boot down
on a puddle and drops gush up

It is astonishing to be
alive, we say, which means
it is astonishing to be here
among these future dead

I spill into the Prater
walk the Hauptallee
I come here often enough to know

each night at five the horses come
tugging their carriages
back from the city.

I suppose I must remember myself
in order to remember them
as each night they remember

their own slick bodies, cold hooves, their
slack-lipped exhale into winter
all just to know their way home.

The Sound

In an unnamed sound,
a tribe arrive with a waka.
They pull up on the shore of an arched-back island
and see stone eyes peek out from the water.
These eyes belong to an old god's
boat, long since sunk and turned to stone.
                        Some thousand years and a ship slips by,
the HMS Pelorus. The men on the ship name
the sound in its honour, and later people
plant pines, walk inland
through drowned river valleys.
            A girl, struggling over rocks, asks what's in the
                sound's name,
and her father who likes to have answers tells her
long before it was Pelorus
it was the shattered prow of the old gods' waka.
Why did it sink she says but he's not sure. Only the girl
            still sees whipped foam for lashes
round stone eyes that blink with each slow wave.
And Pelorus was a ship, the father's saying, that's
an old name too. A Sicilian peninsula, crowned
by Mt Etna, and underneath
Hephaestus and his forge, where everything
is burned, molten and remade.

The girl leaps down from the rocks
and she and the stone eyes stare up at the man.
Everything? she says.
Everything, the man says.

In Time

That city we let our thoughts pour into.
That winter we combed our hair till it fell
and we wondered, alone, how to cure death.
The spring the deer came
and filled the parks, ear-against-ear.
The fall leaves fell the colour of rabbits
and bees bumped inside our cheeks.
The winter you felt had just left when it came back white-
masked, crying.
That summer.
That unseasonable feeling of something approaching
as the car crawls over the horizon line, and its wheels
slide from its metal body, to reveal its wings, to fly.

The Lever

I spend hours as a gambler shovels coins
in whatever currency we keep

letting all our hours sleep
in the unbreakable brains of our machines.

When I pull the lever I know the lever.

I know each second before each second knows
me, but while I think this doubles me

I'm halved. When I pull
the lever I know the lever

pulls me; so I say the lever
has to do with love; because I want

to know you but know your being
makes me half-sad you're wholly here,

half-happy. I'm here to collect matter
that will let us build a new life. Still;

as the advertisements know,
there's nothing to it.

I ask for one more day, and it comes.

Fourteen Mistakes

'You never reach any truth without making fourteen mistakes'

Razumikhin, drunk in *Crime and Punishment*

1.
How we learned to create a thunderclap
in a lab with dust and mirrors

How we designed a clap to blast
away every echo

2.
How we moved to new cities
and wrote our addresses in loose font
on the back of every envelope from
every drawer in every office we visited from Auckland to
    Brooklyn to Hackney

and spoke our names
only with accents formed
in locales we'd lately visited
so no one could guess what we were

3.

How we drizzled cold grease between
our fingers till we forced what we touched

to gleam

4.

And I sewed you into an old sweater
worn so bare it was no longer cotton

but two life-sized holes

5.

How we posed for an unseen creature
as we imagined it shifting
between trees trying

to steal a better look

6.

(How desperate we were not to recall
the horrors of ourselves)

7.
(And how the echoes kept arriving
like swallows crashing

against windowpanes
trying to make glass air)

8.
How we baked silence
behind glass

till it warmed and grew

9.
And when an architect asked
to build a garden inside us

we pried ourselves open and let him in
until we were filled with paths and gates
we did not own the maps for

10.
And when we realised the architect had left for good
how proud we were still to've been
an acciaccatura to his chord

11.
How in the mornings we woke, still drunk,
with rain pattering the windows,
and mist draped through trees,
waiting for our old brains to wake

12.
And when we finally admitted
we wanted to go home
we couldn't be re-admitted

till we re-mapped our own insides
found the end of every path
crafted a key for each gate

and acted cured
of all we'd claimed to know

13.

And by the time we could see

we were doomed

it was winter.

14.

And we drove to the edge of our adopted city
rubbed salt in our tires
threaded snow through our fingers
and listened to the melting layers

of all we hadn't done
the towns we wouldn't visit
the people we'd never meet
and let it all trickle around us like music.

The Fall

What William felt for a yellow-haired girl, I felt till I heard
the furniture fall
during gravity's return

when the planets settled
and silence translated
to siren

Maud knew only ill love lasts
and the sisters dreamed of unlonely Moscow

even if this repeats it will still be first light,
first thought, the rubble of stones that clack against flood
the gap-between-teeth of sea-through-rocks

Tolstoy knows the cast of the world's show
and Flaubert knows how to walk and catch
a-mind-at-sprint, in word-pour, as his curtain creaks open on
      day

and what William felt for a yellow-haired girl
was what's felt for a known ghost
and only Maud knew ill love lasts

but is there nothing better
for the brain or ear
than the song? For the brain

or ear, what William felt for a yellow-haired girl, I felt till I
      heard
the furniture fall
during gravity's return – which made

song – when the planets settled
and silence translated
to siren

so we learned only ill love lasts
and followed, unlovely, to Moscow

The Hold I Have

The hold I have's not one I want to lose
though it's caught in the flick of the clock through this blood
which knows it can't gulp down tides, can't tear out time,
needs a rest from the world I have wrinkled
in fingers, questions, musics. I try to teach my breath a new north,
    new east,
but the man in our town is still out by the graves, and he waits
for the horse or car or woman who will bring me to his dirt.
If you see them come, warn them I plan
to sing my way out.

Centre Strange

I shift into centre strange   gears lift

I am the cloak raised   to show you dressed as a lion

with no voice   in this year since the quake

since the buildings gave   way to water

the fields remembered to flood with milk   and you were thirsty

I forgive you   for itched blossom   for fallen fruit

I'd make up stories to get home too

I'd light my lanterns till they grew to garden

and stay in that garden till I changed

Born Breathing

Because I have never quite caught the moment when you
stand and breathe on top of a mountain in a country where
you were born, and

because I have never been trapped in an underground cavern
with a single candle and no water, and

because a man I was once in love with just sent me a
photograph from Colorado of a famous man's baby booties
and his gold death mask,

and because he was so gentle I had to push him away,
and because *because* means by cause of, and causes multiply *as
a matter of course*, and because our arguments come to us like
breath,

I am trying to keep the seconds still, in this bed overlooking a
window blasted white by mist

while I look on the dark web for a definition of the seconds
after a wisdomflash, where

you re-see each tip of tree, each gasping leaf, each scrape of
thin snow, when

your naked, foolish self can't be argued with, and

your death mask is, for that second, wiped clean.

The Heads

At the heads the waves crash rage at rocks and you watch,
you stretch your attention like it can't snap.
There are songs stuck in you that you might hum when your
light's snuffed, when your tree's cut, neck's split.
When the metaphors eat the real.
But how will you sing when your brain's gone? Here's how;
when you die, don't think of the mind, but feel how your
body is.
For if creasing's strange, why not uncreasing.
Why not chrysalis.
Why not as your brain discovers second childhood, your body
forgets its markings too.
Why not bonelessness can mumble song.
I've not thought to ask if heaven has seasons or how I might
be cured of my need for new, but in my city the sun has come
out for the first time in weeks and it knows how long since
I've spoken to a man or woman.
And it says you must go and find some park bench with a
plaque to a local who loved the sparrows, and you must carve
their name into a napkin and let it go in the wind.
You cannot mourn all the dead, it says.
You must let them go one by one.

Home

Hills gasped in bursts. Glass door
takes sun in its mouth, spits it back.
Swings open and slides my reflection

off its surface. While I'm leaving
again these dark hills, their light-string's threaded
through me; I see them

in every skyline. I hear them called
names, spoken in German. I smell
them damp and crushed in my hand.

I hold wrinkled rivers, ocean's fuss,
rumble, hills a string
of balding heads, and

sky's thin slice above – young sky!

It is always the year I leave.

And in 1947 my father is always traveling
with his father from their bombed-out London
life to a pinprick on the map called

Norfolk Island. They are driven from the airport
in the island's only taxi. They get out
and their new kind of England

is empty. My father,
a child, finds a trail of white buttons
like speech bubbles

leading down to shore.

Epilogue

I'm not here to repair the world.
No one here's here for much, except
perhaps these high windows boasting sky.
My friend says love is easier the less
you know a person. The more you know
the less you love. I say love's
an exhausted word, used for everything.
I turn the tap on, cold, the stream smooth,
and I can't remember why in Hell
I should turn it off.
Doesn't language get tired?
Doesn't it get sick of
lulling us into believing
all the **** we say? In the Prater a willow dips herself
into water and stirs her own image, and
in the lake her leaves refract, refuse to repair.
Isn't love also the kind of cruelty
you give to someone because you can't hold
all that cruelty in your own hands?
All I know's I'm overflowing.
All I know's I'm overflowing and I'm not sure
how much of me the world can hold.

Maker

Home's far and grown old. A friend gives
birth in three hours in a snowstorm
on the floor of a flat in Camberwell.

Poppy Wotherspoon, born in snow.

I walk with a pen and futures I tried to have
and couldn't. Not to want a child but to not
later want to've wanted.

Keep it simple so: Went out walking in Berlin
with wet hair, and realized through a year all grief'd
dried. And winter burst in.

Sing then the might haves. Sing the death not sought.
Sing so much seeking. Interrupting – after some months
enter a new character – and why this one, why him?

Because a particularly snowed-in winter, because
a friend's disappointment, because two young peacocks
     pecking
at a rubbish dump?

Because, the child says, confidently. Be cause.

Of course. East.
Of course, then, myself, with gloves left at home,
knuckles bloodless and greed eyed.

Know fragility's needed, is what makes us whole.
I missed this lightness. Who had it when I didn't?
A fire hydrant's red's

the exact brightness. At Tempelhofer Feld,
black dogs beside crows. In my old life we made a lot
and it took so much to pull apart; makeshift gardens

grown and changed, bare twigs stuck up like
hair, and now even in winter couples perch
on the edge of wooden boxes, calling out hallo

and smiling at strangers. My fingers form warmth slowly
out of coatpockets. Again I see
that rogue loveliness in dirt. Let's put our feet down

flat, chart patterns in soil. Let's take pen,
work ink. Think a female Buck Mulligan,
think a cold charlatan, think a warm-nighted man.

Think I'll make makers before meeting mine.

Acknowledgements

Thank you to the editors of publications where these poems previously appeared: *And Other Poems*, *Five Dials*, *IKA*, *Landfall*, *Lyrikline*, *Mslexia*, *NZEPC*, *Oxford Poetry*, *Poetry London*, *Poetry@Sangam*, *The Rialto*, and *SchlossPost*. Some of these poems also appeared in *Blaue Stunde* (Edition Solitude, 2016). I'm very grateful for the support of Akademie Schloss Solitude, Can Serrat, Creative New Zealand, the Grimshaw Sargeson Trust, Massey University, and the Michael King Writers' Centre.

Many, many thanks to Deryn Rees-Jones for her perception and patience, and to so many others who've helped me on this odd road: Katy Dion, Bill Manhire, Ranjit Hoskote, Eirik Høyer Leivestad, Chelsea Wald, Fotini Lazaridou-Hatzigoga, Bradley Harrison Smith, Laura Kaye, Mark Leidner, Sam Gaskin, Steven Whiting, Eric and Simone Whiting, Alison Welsby, Sam Elworthy, Anna Hodge, the staff, fellows, and football players of Solitude – and finally, to Suzy, Mandy, Peter, Vere, Polly, Mike, Zoë, Alie, Lily, little Pete, and Ada.

ARTS COUNCIL
NEW ZEALAND TOI AOTEAROA
creative*nz*